A Sustainable Karate-ka

A Small Book About a Long Journey

Scott Langley

MASON PUBLISHING

First published in 2022 by
Mason Press
Rear of Cullenswood Park
Ranelagh
Dublin 6]

Amazon paperback ISBN: 978 1 78846 263 1
eBook ISBN: 978-1 78846 262 4

Cover design by Gareth Jones, www.gazjonesdesign.com
Typesetting and layout by Dinky Typesetting and Design

Contents

	Introduction	6
One	*Don't get fat, inflexible, or unfit*	13
Two	*Respect coaches; just don't let them lead*	18
Three	*Grade within the margin*	23
Four	*You are never in a position of power, only responsibility*	29
Five	*Zero-sum game thinking*	33
Six	*Enforced austerity*	37
Seven	*Karate adventures*	41
Eight	*Don't be myopic*	45
Nine	*Karate isn't a thing; a karate-ka is*	51
Ten	*Axiomatic judgement*	56
Eleven	*Have a good foundation*	60
Twelve	*Teach to the generation below*	65
Thirteen	*Have an inefficient, sustainable system*	70
Fourteen	*You ain't all that, Scott!*	74
	Postscript	80

Introduction

In many walks of life, it is possible to see people who have spent years working hard and rising to a position of power only to ebb out their remaining career desperately clinging on to what they had achieved – I guess that is normal. Whether it be a middle-management tyrant, an ageing academic or a formidable secretary, all can share the common trait of putting their energy into defending their position. Once-dynamic and hard-working individuals who pushed themselves – and maybe those around them – now refocus their efforts and attentions on protecting and bolstering their territory and maintaining the status quo. I doubt you would find the same number of people following a similar approach within the world of self-employed tradespeople or serial entrepreneurs. No, this self-cocooning within the structure of our work lives is the preserve of those who find themselves in large institutions: multi-national companies, the civil service, universities.

It's not all employees, of course, not even a majority, but maybe a small minority and the efforts they put into what they protect is in no way connected to the amount they have. We have all been frustrated by a 'jobsworth' whose sole responsibility it is to stamp a certain document or press a certain button. One's progress to more important things is hampered and delayed by one individual who wields an incredibly small, yet vital, amount of power with great effect. At moments like this we must make a choice either to step back, take a deep breath and give the person their moment of control. Or grab them by the throat, drag them across the counter and slap them into compliance ... I hope, for the most part, that we choose the former rather than later.

My point is, I think we are all born with a certain amount of energy and fight within us. Coming from a male perspective (as I only can), in our twenties and thirties it is all about slaying the dragon and in our forties and fifties it is about saving the maiden. And I think our working lives may be intricately entwined with this idea. The initial building of a career may eventually lead to an easing off the gas pedal followed by a certain amount of coasting to the finish line ... But I can hear the reader ask, 'What has this got to do with karate?'

I am glad you asked.

For the best part of two decades I have travelled the world teaching our beloved art. I have taught in massive sports halls to hundreds of black belts, I have taught in small private dojos to half a dozen enthusiasts. I have taught on dirt in the slums of India and in some of the most impressive, purpose-built dojos inside and out of Japan. I have seen it all and enjoyed every minute. Within my travels I have met certain kinds of people, archetypes of the karate world, if you will. Of course, I will paint a picture using broad-brush strokes, referring to no one in particular ... Although you know who you are!

The one type that stands out for me is the slightly ageing, generally (but not exclusively) male, karate-ka who is a little overweight, teaches most of the time and stands around watching my class with the pretence that they are 'assisting'. Generally, they are the head of the dojo, the main instructor. In fact, often is the case that they started the dojo many years ago and, in some cases, they have built up a huge student base. They are the quintessential karate-ka, having trained for decades, achieved a high rank and produced countless good students. However, look closer and they lack that enthusiasm that they must have once had. Their dogi does not look like it has seen any sweat for many years and once the pristine karate suit has been removed, they just look *average* … possibly the worst insult you could hurl at any karate-ka.

For me, this class of karate-ka is the middle-management, older academic, formidable secretary of the karate world. Once, I am sure, they worked hard. Most would have received a credible Dan ranking from a credible organisation. At some point, I must presume, they were good enough to achieve Shodan, Nidan, even Sandan. But that may have been some time ago. Fast-forward three decades and these karate-ka now claim to have been training for forty years. The truth is, however, that they trained hard for ten years and then taught for the remaining time. This is a very different situation. That pool of knowledge they had gained through diligent work suddenly becomes finite. Depending what group they are with, their rank may no longer be associated with their actual karate level, so these instructors could be godan or rokudan, maybe even higher, but they are still teaching the same lessons they had learnt decades before. Furthermore, as their karate hasn't been simmering along over this period, they have actually moved backwards (Funakoshi Sensei did warn us about this). Maybe they have a Sandan level of understanding, but their bodies can no longer physically articulate that conceptual knowledge.

As their own students approach the level that they peaked at, instructors' egos may be challenged, their power threatened. And without fail, the more a person aligns with this archetype, the more mentally inflexible, the less dynamic and the more jobsworth they become. I once had a pot-bellied, decrepit ignoramus of an instructor deride my karate because I didn't know the number of moves in Bassai Dai. For him (and maybe the international group that he belonged to) knowing the count of each kata and the kiai points was paramount. Being fit, flexible and strong enough to do the kata well obviously was not.

My point is, these instructors seem to have had a certain amount of energy, fire in the belly, to push themselves to a certain level. Once there, they became comfortable in the position of power, they eased off on the sweating and physical demands of karate, teaching instead of training, believing they are the same.

So, how does this affect me? As mentioned before, I have been travelling, first assisting and then teaching, since my early twenties. It has been part of my life for almost as long as I can remember, yet it was only in my late twenties that I started to notice this archetype. I had just finished an intensive five-year training period in Japan. Exhausted and, frankly, sick of certain aspects of karate, I looked at these instructors and thought, *Is this my future?* For sure, a certain enthusiasm I had had for karate had been obliterated. The question was, could the fuel of that fire be replenished? Or was I destined to be old, fat and inflexible in line with my peer group? At the same time I have, from an early age, felt that I was a person prone to the extremes. I could easily become obsessive about anything. As a kid, I remember watching on TV the SAS storm the Iranian embassy in London – the newsflash interrupted my post-school cartoons – and instantly absorbing every bit of information about the regiment. (They actually started producing kids' SAS annuals every Christmas – merry Christmas! Here, read about some trained killers!)

When I started playing hockey, that too became an obsession. Before I had my own stick, I found an old 2x4, cut the end at a slight angle and practised dribbling with some random ball. I would do it for hours in my room with the result that within a season, I was a level above most and eventually played in a national league with members of the British U21 squad on my team. Of course, shortly after falling in love with hockey I also started karate and this is where my greatest obsession began. I made the spare room into a dojo.

After destroying several age-appropriate punchbags, my parents got me a Lonsdale bag. My sensei gave me a freestanding makiwara as well. So, from about fourteen until I left for university at nineteen, whenever I wasn't in the regular dojo, you would find me in my dojo. During summer holidays my routine was a thirty- to forty-minute run in the mornings, an hour session in my dojo at lunchtime (bag-work and makiwara) and then each evening a two-hour session at one of the two local dojos. It was relentless and haphazard, but ultimately fruitful. It made me strong. I remember returning to school after the summer break between GCSEs and A Levels, when I was sixteen. A combination of this training regime and a sudden and dramatic dump of puberty hormones on my slightly feeble and squeaky body had changed me, developed me, built me anew.

But was this level of training sustainable? At the time, maybe, long term, no. Later, in Japan, I met kids that had, at the age of fourteen, entered karate junior high schools. They had trained six hours per day, six days a week. They had gone on to similar high schools with similar training regimes. They had concluded this marathon by entering a karate university and, again, trained six hours per day, six days a week. At the age of twenty-two, some would ceremonially burn their dogi; most never did karate again. That drive, that determination, that energy to push themselves forward was finite and spent well before it ought to have been – although it had often resulted in spectacular competition success.

During the same period, I was training three to four hours per day, but arriving in Japan after university, I still wanted more. After learning about the pitfalls of training to this intensive level, it struck me that maybe I should take a more sustainable approach to karate.

I left Japan in July 2002. I flew to LA and spent a month travelling from coast to coast before flying back home for another month of home-cooked goodness. I then went to India for a month, teaching karate and meditating with the large Buddhist community there. During that period I met up with friends and family, sempai and sensei. I received a bit of sempai advice from Richard Amos. 'Don't get fat', he said. I received further advice from another sempai, Phil Freeman. 'Don't become an alcoholic' was his guidance. By the time I moved to Ireland in October 2002 I was, thankfully, recharged and ready, but mindful that whatever I decided to do to push myself forward, I had to make sure that it was sustainable. That is to say, if I decided to introduce an element into my obsessive regime, I had to be sure that it would be something I could do for ever – no small task indeed. At the same time, that fire in my belly, replenished by three months of relaxation, couldn't be spent rapidly. It would be there for when I felt lazy, tired, or bored of the drudgery of training. I had to develop a regime that I could stick to, tweak and evolve if necessary, and then, when necessary, plug in this fire to push me forward only when needed. For me, this was the sustainable approach that I would need to never allow all my hard work to be squandered by laziness and a love of cake and beer!

I moved to Ireland twenty years ago. A bit of a milestone. My sustainable path has had a lot of troughs and peaks, cul-de-sacs and wrong turns. I have had some interesting experiences and learnt a lot. It is these experiences that I wish to confess now. In my dojo I have young, talented karate-ka, some professional, others amateurs, all of them lifers: they are in it for the long haul. Around the world there are countless dojos with countless karate-ka of a similar ilk. I hope my thoughts are at least entertaining, if not useful. Therefore, what follows are the guidelines that I try to adhere to 95 per cent of the time. Most are instinctual, this being the first time I have actually tried to grab the jumble of thoughts running through my head and distil them onto paper. Over the years, this process has evolved through necessity. Some thoughts deal with my body's inclination to being fat; others, my ego's desire to be in control. Some thoughts are about power, others about insecurity. Above all else, they are ideas that I have thought deeply about. Some may speak to you, the others you can ignore. Either way, I hope that you too can find a sustainable path.

ONE

Don't get fat, inflexible, or unfit

I train Tuesday, Wednesday and Thursday mornings. It's tough. There are plenty of videos online of the morning crew huffing and puffing our way through the monotonous, mundane and monstrous training regime. Back in my thirties, my working week would be teaching away Saturday and Sunday (forty to forty-five weekends per year), teaching seventeen classes Monday to Thursday and training three mornings per week. Fridays and Mondays I would be mostly travelling. So Thursdays, after morning training, I would be at my most tired.

There was a baker on the walk home from the dojo. I would buy two large Cornish pasties (a rare treat in Ireland) and two large cream doughnuts. I would go home, scoff the lot and fall into a carb coma until I had to force my tired body into compliance to teach the four Thursday-evening classes. It was a tough schedule, but I was building a dojo, a group and a family. It had to be done. However, as I approached forty, my once manageable belly was no longer so manageable. With horror, I looked down after tying my obi one day and was unable to see the knot over my Cornish-pasty gut. For a while I convinced myself that I was fit, strong and trained regularly, so it was impossible to have a belly; this was surely an aberration. However, reality always has a way of slapping you in the face and my seemingly shrinking belt and hibernating knot did that. This was not what I wanted. Something had to be done.

This was when people were starting to talk about intermittent fasting. At about that time Michael Mosley's *Horizon* documentary ('Eat, Fast and Live Longer') aired. I watched it with interest and began the regime straight away. Twice a week I would only have 600 calories, the rest of the time I could eat what I want. It had immediate results. It was tough, but I managed. I lost the desired weight and my belt returned to an appropriate length, but as the pounds shed, so too did my desire to fight the hunger pains. So, I switched to the five-day, 16/8 version. That is, I fasted sixteen hours per day and ate in the remaining eight. Skipping breakfast each morning was easy. Having lunch at midday and dinner before 8 pm was doable and I have done this during the week for the last decade. However, as I approached my fifties, it suddenly wasn't enough. Four years ago, I switched to being vegetarian during the week (most of my regime focuses on weekdays simply because I am away most weekends and at the mercy of my host; they often want to take me to fine steak restaurants and punish me with the delicious red wine). That worked for a while. Three years ago, I started to reduce my lunch size, and now it is mostly a bowl of soup or a salad. During lockdown, I limited my alcohol consumption to twice a week and started taking cold showers in the mornings, a regime I have continued. And recently, through the help of probiotics and the tweaking of my gut biome, I have cut out most refined sugar. For the most part, it works, but still now, if I feel I am getting too heavy, I just fast for 24 hours, going from dinner to dinner, skipping breakfast and lunch. And, yes, it is bloody hard. Not physically, though. I never feel weak during training, my body never screams the rumbling roar of a sugar low. And hunger has a habit of coming and going. Raising its disgruntled head at breakfast and lunchtime, only to disappear for the rest of the day – often vanquished with the aid of a cup of tea. What is tough is the psychological battle. 'Oh, no, not again!' is my weekly mantra as I realise today is the day I need to not eat. These days are farthest from my extreme-prone mind as I say yes to an extra glass of wine or dessert at a fancy restaurant I have been taken to. However, during the week, looking at myself in the mirror during morning training, trying to keep up with the teenagers and twenty-somethings to my right, it all comes crashing home, balance must be and is achieved … and it feels great.

Last summer I spent a week away from home in the company of other instructors. We met for breakfast each morning, where I had a cup of tea and watched them tuck into a fry. On the Saturday I treated myself to a sausage sandwich, a delight, as only sausages, melted butter and toast can be. One of the other instructors looked at me and said, 'I thought you don't eat breakfast?'

'No, I love breakfast,' I replied. 'I just don't eat it during the week.'

'What?' he said. 'You restrict yourself?' A concept he had never heard of, I thought, and which his belly confirmed.

My regime may seem normal for most, hard for some, easy for others. For me, it is just enough (for the time being). If I had, in my early thirties, suddenly decided to incorporate all these guidelines into my life, I would have failed immediately. I may have had a six-pack, but very little else in my life. For me, it has been about incremental change as and when necessary, rather than a massive, dramatic change long after it was needed. By making small changes, I started a process of monitoring and tweaking my life in order to facilitate what I wanted: to not get fat.

Each person has their challenges and for me, this is it. Others can substitute fat with fitness, stamina, strength, flexibility etc. Whatever it is, we have to put a lot of work into warding off our natural enemy. Plus, that work has to be constantly tweaked, changed and re-thought over the years. I watch, read and absorb information that helps me deal with my body and its natural tendencies to sabotage my journey. And whichever demon we face, it is true to say that for all of us, post-mid-thirties we are in decline. We may already be in that mindset of believing teaching is the same as training. I am sure we can convince ourselves that we are not weakening by throwing out a fast punch or kick to a stationary lower grade. However, the decline is inevitable and already progressing. For some, by the time they have a level of self-realisation, the task of returning to some level of fitness is so huge that denial is the easier option.

I found that the sustainable way is to make small, incremental decisions early, before it is too late. Getting used to not eating breakfast in my thirties was much easier than losing twenty pounds of fat in my forties. After all, without a healthy, fit, flexible body to work with, my journey through the landscape of karate would be almost impossible.

Teaching in France during the pandemic, always finding a way.

TWO

Respect coaches; just don't let them lead

I hope you don't think I am advocating the idea that if you are fat, unfit, or inflexible you can't play an active role in the dojo. No, of course not. I don't want to fat-shame a generation of karate instructors and banish them to the sidelines of village halls and sports centres (I only apply those harsh rules to my own life). In what other 'sport' would we expect the 'coach' to be the fittest and strongest on the pitch, court, or field? Soichi Sakamoto, a Hawaiian-born science teacher, revolutionised the coaching of swimming, introducing interval and resistance training into the sport. He had the goal of taking novice students up to Olympic standard within three years; something he did with great success, with three Olympic medals and countless national and international titles showered upon his stable of elite swimmers.

I mention this here because he also couldn't swim.

My point is, in any other physically intensive pastime, sport, or hobby the onus is never on the instructor or coach to be physically on top of their game. That is not to say some aren't, it just isn't necessary. When success is solely judged on the outcome or results of a match or race, if the coach can touch their toes or not or how quickly they can run is beside the point. Having an analytical mind, seeing the strengths and weakness and, most importantly, being able to push, inspire and motivate the athlete to achieve their personal goals is a real skill that should never be devalued.

I can teach well but I am a terrible coach. I naturally score high on pattern recognition and can quickly see connections between elements of karate. I use that skill to develop lessons and training regimes that give people the best possible chance to improve. Once I have delivered that knowledge, it is kind of up to them. Of course, I care that they improve and am happy when they do well, but I lack the ability to push them and motivate them in a one-to-one manner. I have, for example, never wanted to coach the the national squad in Ireland, yet I have met many great coaches. Some are good at karate, others aren't. Regardless, their students are great. Generally, that success is limited to the competition end of the karate spectrum and some readers may deride that as a small and insignificant element of our art. Still, competing is a great way to give students short-term goals while physically pushing them hard. Therefore, I would never underestimate the value and worth of individuals like this in one's dojo. In my experience, every Japanese dojo that I know well has a number of these characters within their ranks. They wear pristine dogi during class, they carry clipboards around at competitions, and they are often the first to give support and guidance to the young and dedicated karate-ka that populate the dojo. Are they good at karate? Are they tough, strong, and fearsome? I suspect not. They do, however, carry a different type of respect from the students. They must have reached a good level at some point, and the black belt around their waist speaks to this. Now I suspect most can't touch their toes nor drum up the fortitude to endure a tough kumite session, but they are a vital part of the community of the dojo and have their solid, well-earned place within its ranks – they are true sensei. They offer guidance not only to the students, but also the head sensei, being able to read the room in a way that the instructor may be unable to. Knowing the ebb and flow of the athletes' moods and motivation gives them an insight that may be lacking within the sensei, yet is beneficial to the leadership of the class. So, no, I am not advocating that, unless you are a super-fit, extraordinary example of your demographic, you must throw away your dogi and never again disgrace the hallowed walls of the dojo with your soft-skinned feet.

Should this type of sensei lead the dojo? Absolutely not! This sort of instructor can often end up directing a dojo along a path that may not be best for the students. Rather than having a vital, yet supportive role, once this type of instructor starts to make decisions about significant elements of the training regime or technical direction, once they start to lead classes, but are unable to gain any level of authority based on skill, it can lead to disastrous results.

Over the years, I have experienced teaching at dojos headed by such instructors. Of course, they would not have invited me to teach. Mostly, I would have been invited by the number two of the dojo. You can tell as soon as you walk into the venue, there is a slight unease that fills the air. The broad brushstrokes are that the lead sensei (rotund, late middle-aged, been training – aka teaching – for years) has been convinced by a number of his young guns in the dojo to get this Scott Langley (or any other professional instructor) to come and teach. I do my thing while the chap waddles around the back, 'assisting'. It mostly leads to disastrous results. The younger, more active swathe of the dojo loves the class, the energy and the ideas, while the older, senior instructor hates it, seeing what I do as a threat. It often leads to the dojo splitting, with the junior instructors going their own way, no longer wanting to have their path defined by an instructor who long ago found his[1] own path to have led to a cul-de-sac. It is an obvious, but not inevitable, conclusion of someone wanting to continue to have karate be part of their life but who is unable to see any other model except run a dojo, be the sensei, dictate all elements of the community.

I often think another scenario could have been played out. Before the senior instructor stagnated, they could have passed the dojo along. Slowly, over time, as the junior black belts became more experienced, they could have been given more responsibility, even been encouraged to go out and learn new ideas and bring them back to the community. This may have even prolonged the life of the senior instructors' enthusiasm. Either way, it would have allowed the old silver-back to bow out gracefully, morphing into a senior mentoring role, and watch with pride as the next generation continues to build upon what they originally started.

This may seem utopian at best, grossly naive at worst. But when you consider that the vast majority of karate instructors teach as a hobby, the only thing they receive from their hours of work is pride, prestige and respect. They don't need to keep control of the dojo to earn a living and pay their mortgage, so allowing the community to develop in this manner will only continue to deepen their standing within the group. This is the most sustainable way to keep a dojo going, and I wish

1. I use the possessive pronoun here consciously. Without being too cliched, this pattern of behaviour seems, on the whole, to be the reserve of the male ego. ☹

many instructors considered it before it is too late, the young guns in the dojo become frustrated, fractures happen and the ageing instructors finish their karate journey alone … I paint a sad picture, but I have seen it many times.

Japan 2020, with two formidable instructors at the Shorinji Kempo Headquarters in Japan.

THREE

Grade within the margin

Kyu and Dan gradings are a complete nightmare. I have watched with horror and tried to arbitrate more arguments about grading rights and results than any other issue. Apart from the money involved, one problem is that, when it comes to awarding a rank, there are no absolutes – anyone who says otherwise is deluding themselves … or lying. I have met *yudansha* who have been awarded senior rank from the most prestigious associations, yet their karate knowledge has as much depth as a toddler's paddling pool. And I have met young black belts from independent, insular and anything other than mainstream groups who have been terrific, talented, and knowledgeable about many aspects of karate.

Gone are the days when there was a gold standard within the Shotokan world, where having three initials after your rank meant everything and those without this specific triad were scorned as being illegitimate, even fraudulent. This overly controlled, super-stringent regulation of rank promotion in essence backfired and delegitimised itself. What followed was a period of post-modernism. What I mean by that is the belief that if you thought you were good enough, you were. Born from the repercussion of draconian institutions who, for far too long, sought to maintain power over those they governed, the subjugated revolted and tore down the frameworks of control that were once thought essential. Taking a wider perspective, for similar reasons it bubbled up elsewhere in society and culture, manifesting in different ways. Former respected pillars of society are no longer trusted: teachers blamed for kids' dwindling grades; doctors second-guessed by patients with the aid of Dr Google; and politicians vilified and mistrusted before they even open their mouths.

The result in karate was people started awarding themselves Dan grades left, right and centre. It became a free-for-all: if you had done your time and thought yourself worthy of an hachidan, well you should jolly well award yourself one! The Three-Initial gang derided it as dishonest, even illicit in some way. They failed to see that this was their doing. Awarding a favoured few with high ranks and the trappings and privileges that go with that while turning a blind eye to equally (or more) talented karate-ka was bound to lead to unrest. Besides, how did Nakayama Sensei get his hachian? Funakoshi Sensei was only godan when he died. In fact, Nakayama Sensei graded to Sandan in 1951, but was Hachidan by 1961. Not for a moment do I think he didn't deserve that rank, but awarding yourself high grades certainly is not unheard of – or the reserve of the West.

I have heard countless stories and witnessed senior Japanese instructors travelling abroad to conduct an examination only to fail everyone because they lacked a certain *Je ne sais quoi*, or as they would say '*ma, chotto dame da ne!*'

For students, months and years of dedicated training, days of stress and anxiety and a considerable amount of money dismissed with a 'no, fail … next time'. There was always going to be a backlash, especially when these *clients*, having paid a considerable amount of money for a *product* that was denied them, looked around and saw other, arguably lesser karate-ka wearing black belts, some holding quite high rank. They realised how arbitrary the whole system was and, therefore, how prone it could be to the whims and caprices of the visiting instructor. These large associations, having become a tad dismissive of their community through their own hubris, may have brought it upon themselves. Once these monoliths of the karate world had their one true power – the ability to legitimate a grade – shattered, their foundations started to crumble.

If you have watched the film *The Big Short*, you will remember the great scene where certain nerdy analysts recognise the emergence of a small pattern of defaults from the NINJA (no income/no job) mortgages. They extrapolate that out to realise the banking sector is a house of cards, flimsier than many of the prefab trailers that had been bought by the NINJA loans. In a rare moment, they realised the future was predictable and inevitable.

I bring that up because I sometimes wonder if ever there was a similar executive meeting in any of the major karate organisations in the world. When Kanazawa Sensei broke from the JKA and took enough members worldwide to create the SKIF, was there any soul-searching within the headquarter offices in Ebisu? When there were major splits in almost every country in the world, did anyone sit down and say 'I think I see the emergence of a trend'? For sure, not all of the fractures seen throughout the karate world are due to grades being awarded or the ability to award rank, but that is undeniably part of it.

So, how can a sustainable karate-ka approach such a

matter? In most groups in Japan, instructors are allowed to grade three grades below them. Maybe an examiner has to attend a course or write a report, but Yondan can grade to Shodan, Godan can grade to Nidan, Nidan can even grade to 1st kyu. It's the way it is. I would argue that once this basic premise is done away with, trouble starts to happen, the rot starts to set in. We all know of groups where only one or two at the top control all gradings, not only dan gradings, but kyu as well. Instructors who, historically, happened to be at the right place at the right time and were doing kyu examinations when they were shodan and nidan level, now (as hachidan) insist that in order to be a kyu examiner you must be X, Y or Z (criteria that the countless godan, rokudan and nanadan don't fulfil). It does not take a genius to realise that these decisions, the hoops that are created for junior instructors to jump through, are driven by financial reasons. Hardly the epitome of budo. Senior grades ignoring the essence of the dojo kun, the moral code that they often pontificate about during class. No matter how long it may take, this path will ultimately lead to disaster. Like *The Big Short*, where a number of insightful individuals ran the numbers, *did the maths* and realised that no matter how small the trickle, the movement was in one direction. A family here and a family there failing to pay their mortgage may seem insignificant while the rest of the company is making record profits. However, if the business is only trending in one direction, the model is completely unsustainable, the consequences are inevitable.

These giants of the karate world are the same. Due to split after split, once-monolithic monopolies of the karate would have been fragmented and broken, becoming rubble of their former selves. Karate is not a business, but if you looked at large groups with a business eye, you would be horrified to see a 70 per-cent, 80 per-cent, even 90 per-cent reduction in membership and revenue in a ten-, twenty- or thirty-year period. You would have to be blinded by your own arrogance and chutzpah to not notice this trend. Maybe worse, if you do see it, your response would be to double down on your behaviour, your rules and regulations. This, I am afraid, is not a sustainable way to run a group.

I would also like to add another idea. It should be taken for granted that an instructor can grade three ranks below them. I also think there should be a limit on how many grades you can grade below you. A Hachidan grading people for Shodan? Sure, that's fine, but I think there is a possibility of losing touch when you are that far removed from the grade you are judging. A Yondan in the same situation is still deeply connected to the process of becoming Shodan, the physical struggle to reach one's potential. That investment made is still forefront in the memory of the examiner. This informs their decision. For a Hachidan, that effort is a distant recollection. I think at the very least, very senior grades should always have lower-grade examiners on the test panel to help inform and balance decisions that are made about candidates going to the initial black-belt levels. Many times I have been convinced, even overruled by a majority decision, to fail a student that I thought should pass. Younger, junior examiners, unafraid to declare their independent position, have rejected my take on the situation and concluded the candidate 'is capable of more'. Karate-ka challenging themselves to gain that coveted black belt are asked to 'try again' at a date sometime in the future and a detailed description of what needs to be done in the meantime is given. It is a constant reminder, a constant safety-valve that keeps the whole process insulated from the vagaries of my own ego.

With Ross Stewart at the HDKI Headquarters.

FOUR

You are never in a position of power, only responsibility

I have been running an international karate group since I was a 29-year-old Yondan. At that time, we had two dojo in England and three dojo in Ireland – just about international. A decade later, the group had over 120 dojo spread out over five nations (all four nations of the United Kingdom and the Republic of Ireland) – definitely international.[1] At the time, we were one of the biggest single-style groups in the UK and the largest association within the JKS and, for most, it appeared that, as the 'head', I wielded a lot of power.

Yet even at my most self-indulgent moments, I never believed I had power. Influence, maybe, but not power. Power is an illusion that people use to cover the cracks of their ego and we wield it at our peril. So, over the years of leading the JKS GB & Ireland, WTKO GB & Ireland and now the HDKI, I have learnt that being in charge means that you

1. For those scratching their head at the complexity of the United Kingdom and Republic of Ireland, I suggest you search for CGP Grey and United Kingdom on YouTube. It'll be five minutes and fifteen educational seconds that you won't regret.

have to allow people to do things that you don't necessarily want them to do.

Contrary to what it may appear from the outside, being the head means that you are constantly shrugging your shoulders and reluctantly saying 'yeah … I guess that's okay'. Why did I reach this conclusion? I think as a young instructor trying to build a national and international group, I had to find a new model of management. Before me, many great and powerful instructors had led groups, often with an iron fist. It was their way or the highway. Rules seemed arbitrary and were often draconian. For a time, it had worked. They were the gatekeepers of knowledge – if students wanted to learn karate, they had to go through the senior sensei. Follow the rules and have access. Break the rules and be excommunicated and ejected into the cold wasteland of illegitimate karate.

By the time I can along, however, things had changed. The 1990s were littered with acrimonious splits and fragmentations of karate groups, throughout Europe and, I presume, the world. I felt that there were many dojo that wanted to be part of a community with a high level of technical knowledge, but not have to put up with the bovine excrement to access it. I started listening to instructors who seemed responsive to my endeavours. They gave me valuable insight and an understanding about what had led them to leave their original groups. For me, the pattern was obvious, and the pitfalls of a malfunctioning group became easily avoidable.

I tried my best to take a new approach with the recently affiliated JKS dojo, providing a service that their affiliation fees actually paid for. I realised that in order for the group that I headed to be sustainable, I must never use the power that I (and others) occasionally imagine I have. In Japan they often say 自分の株が上がる (*Jibun no kabu ga ageru* – your personal stock is rising.) Basically, the Japanese see power and influence as a personal stock, that is earnt, bought and traded, like any stock on the FTSE 100. Work hard and make good deals, your stock will rise. Do the opposite and your stock will fail. I followed that model, but added a little frugal fiscal responsibility – that is, I spent as little stock as possible. What I mean by this is that, time and time again, I faced dilemmas. An affiliated instructor or club wants me to do something that I am not comfortable with. Do I come down hard on them and refuse their request? Or do I accept my uncomfortableness about the situation and allow them to proceed? Saying no would erode the precious stock I had worked hard to build. Saying yes increases my stock, but maybe niggles at my sensibilities. Of course, being constantly compliant has its own dangers; people may take advantage and ultimately the whole group would suffer. However, I am a firm believer that most people, most of the time, are trying to do the right thing. The key? A little empathy. Trying to understand the myriad of needs and desires that sculpt the decision-making of any individual helped me acquiesce more easily.

I have my limits, of course. Over the years, a number of members and dojo have been expelled from the group or removed from a position of responsibility. It is always done with a heavy heart, but with the greater good in mind. However, as a foundation of all decisions, I remind myself I have no power. Each individual of the HDKI Worldwide is a pocket of autonomous power. As such, they freely give me that authority and can freely take it back at any moment. Realising this reinforces the fact that I have a responsibility to every member, not a power over them. For me, this is the best way to sustainably lead a dojo, a group, a community.

Just because the spotlight is on you, doesn't mean you have power.

FIVE

Zero-sum game thinking

I have lost count of the number of times I have seen and heard instructors who have fallen out with students. The once loyal karate-ka, after many years of diligent training, decides to open their own dojo. This is, almost inevitably, followed by the original, senior instructors ostracising their former student as if this young upstart had publicly challenged them to duel at dawn, the honour of each man at stake.

This response baffles me. Does the older instructor feel that there are a finite number of students, money, respect – or whatever they may take from karate – within a certain geographical area? The younger instructor starts a new dojo, therefore every student they are able to attract is a direct reduction in the number of students that the older instructors will receive? This is classic zero-sum game thinking. Like cutting a cake: the more I take, the less you will receive. In fact, a significant number of new dojo and groups that have joined our community over the years have been as a direct consequence of this type of negative, counter-productive thinking. Little do the senior instructors realise that their attitude often culminates in a self-fulfilling prophecy. The younger instructor, cut off from the community they once had standing in, determinedly builds a new group. Fuelled by their youthful energy, they build a dojo far more successful than the one they were expelled from. Of course, I am painting a picture with very broad-brush strokes. However, it seems obvious that this zero-sum game thinking is the most destructive way to lead a dojo or head a community.

The amount of students, prestige and standing within a group is infinite. Instead of zero-sum game thinking, we should have a win-win state of mind. If a student trains diligently, raising their skills to instructor level, the opening of their own dojo is a natural conclusion. For the senior instructor, this should be affirmation of a job well done, not a challenge, not a rejection, not an abandonment. The senior instructor continues with their role, mentoring, guiding and encouraging the younger instructors, passing on their skills and knowledge not only about karate, but also about how to run, manage and lead a dojo. The new dojo flourishes, the original dojo has a wider community to be part of and all members benefit from different points of view, different people to train with, different classes to attend. There may be a friendly rivalry between the two groups, but no animosity, no destructive ill-feeling. This is a win-win situation – and how little I have seen of it in the karate world!

From the micro to the macro and back again, I have seen it all. Just look for the rivalry that exists on an international level, where a once global association split and split again, producing smaller international groups, all disavowing the others and refusing to allow their members to interact with the other groups (some of whom used to be good friends). Or look for it in small villages, where a once-thriving local dojo split over some nonsense, and now two struggling dojo exit with mutual hatred, sometimes in the same parish hall –

albeit on different nights. It is all too common and often the result of zero-sum game thinking. Instead, win-win thinking has to be the way forward and the most sustainable approach to being a karate-ka. Do things happen that you don't entirely agree with? Yes. Do senior instructors lose some level of control of the group or community that they founded? Yes. But rather that, than be left with no community at all.

I often see this through the lens of parenting. Over the years I have watched my daughter move through the inevitable stages of growing up. As a baby, my wife and I monitored and controlled every aspect of her life. As a toddler, she developed a mind of her own and would scoot off in random directions as the mood took her. We followed after her, ready to catch and protect like any diligent parent would. As she started school, she developed a life completely separate from our family unit, which we could only experience vicariously. Now (as a teenager), there are aspects of her life that we have no knowledge of whatsoever. Not only are we not there to save her, we aren't even aware of what she needs saving from.

We can only hope that the foundation we have given her (skills, knowledge and love) is enough to guide her through these tumultuous years. And, we hope, at some point she will go off and create her own family, of which we will always be an important peripheral part. At no point would I think that the love, enjoyment and adventure in our encapsulated world is finite. It seems a ridiculous thought to have, let alone turn into an action. I would never prevent my daughter from experiencing the fun of life because it could limit how much of it I would have. This seems an absurd and bizarre stance to take; yet it is one that is taken time and again by sensei as their students 'grow up'.

No, in order to be successful and sustainable in the karate

world, we must abandon the zero-sum game thinking and try to see as many things as possible as a win-win.

Rick Hotton Sensei enjoying life after teaching together in Norway.

SIX

Enforced austerity

I am surrounded by youngsters. I used to always be the youngest instructor, in the dojo, on seminars, at camps. Now, with the inevitable ticking of the clock I can no longer claim such things. So while my ageing body tries to pretend to the rest of the dojo that it can still move like my colleagues in their twenties, I often distract myself from the pain of inflammation by becoming an annoyingly clichéd, advice-giving machine. This especially happens when I am forced to watch my colleagues' ability to recover from nights out or weekend camps away. Whereas it now takes me days, if not a full week to recover, they are able to be back on the dojo floor as if no party had ever happened. It is at times like this, fuelled by a potent blend of jealousy and truth, that I insist they must have enforced austerity in their lives.

One of my first instructors was the very talented Sadashige Kato Sensei. He had moved to the UK, via Germany, in the mid-1960s and became a major influence in the development of British karate. I first met him in the mid-1980s, when he was a similar age to what I am now, and he would have a profound impact on my karate path. His talent, technique and teaching style were unsurpassed by anyone I had met then and few I have met since. However, despite his seemingly superhuman body control, speed and timing, I never once saw him train. I went to university fourteen miles from his house with the sole purpose of training with him and during those four years I practically became uchi-deshi … Even then I never saw him train. Added to this, he was always very clear in his approach. 'Scott,' he would say, 'train hard until your thirties and then you never have to train hard again – it will last you a lifetime.' Great, I thought. All I had to do was spend the next decade or so in a constant state of near exhaustion and I would be set for life! So, that's exactly what I did. Ten years later, I returned from Japan, Instructors' Course certificate in hand, ready to relax and reap the rewards of all my hard work.

Fortunately, that little bubble was burst fairly quickly and is the subject matter of an entirely different book. However, whether Kato Sensei was simply a unique physical specimen, a natural athlete who didn't need to hone or develop his skills or a guy coasting to a slow stop, having arrived in the UK with such a head start on all the local karate-ka that it lasted him most of his life, I am unsure. What I do know is that the benefits of my training last for just about as long as it takes for the sweat to dry from my soaked dogi. It is fleeting and ephemeral and must be a constant part of my life. This, for me, is where enforced austerity plays a vital role.

I have written about my ever-shrinking diet. That is one way to enforce austerity in one's life, but (unfortunately) it is not the only way. Of course, what is the point of all of this if you can't have fun? Karate itself is austere and boring. No one is going to score the winning try or become man of the match down at the dojo. People looking for a pleasant pastime should walk on by the dojo entrance. So, why do we do karate? I do it because it makes the rest of life easier. To that end, enforced austerity is the framework of thinking that helps me make the correct choices from which the rest of life tries to distract me. For most people, getting older is a natural, inevitable process. For a karate-ka it is a process we must fight tooth and nail to overcome. *Do not go gentle into that good night,* said Dylan Thomas. We must fight and *rage against the dying light*. This is the task of a sustainable karate-ka, to make that karate adventure last as long as possible. And as time goes by, the only way to do that is to have some enforced austerity.

We all know youth is wasted on the young, but we must be careful that wisdom is not wasted on the old. There is no point is having acquired knowledge and expertise only to have an old, damaged body that is incapable of expressing that knowledge. Of course, to quote Oscar Wilde, *everything in moderation, including moderation*. I certainly don't want to become a warrior monk, forsaking all enjoyment that the world can offer. However, we must heed that little voice, whispering quietly in our ear, ready forever to say, 'Okay, enough now. Time to head home!' Do this more times than not and whatever demon that sits on the other shoulder, drawing you down a path of ruin, can be drowned out by the other, more positive voice.

That demon is an elusive shape-shifter. For some instructors, it is food. I have watched, over the years, their ever-shrinking black belt, until finally there are just two short stubs sprouting from the knot. For others, it is drink. As fun as it is, alcohol will slowly destroy the very tool we need for karate – our body. Yet for others still, it is quite the opposite. Excessive training can cause as much body inflammation as binge-drinking. Some people are forever entering competitions, searching for that short hit of adrenaline when they get affirmation from some corner judge they have never met. Maybe it is a less tangible thing that prods and tickles one's amygdala – money, power, respect. Whatever your pill, for me, I have to make sure I have a little enforced austerity in my life which, at the right time, forbids me having the thing I want. By doing this, the adventure that is my karate journey gains longevity.

Always training.

SEVEN

Karate adventures

What's the point?

'That's it!' I'll sometimes joke. 'I quit karate and I want all my money back!'

I guess it doesn't really work as a joke anymore. Karate is really the only job I have ever had, so quitting and asking for my money back is a tad redundant to say the least. Yet the main question – what's the point? – should always be asked. As the pandemic took away so much from us all, my ability to travel and teach was in the first wave of sacrifices we had to offer up for the common good. In March 2020 the Irish government put us all into lockdown on, appropriately, Friday the 13th. That weekend I was free. The following weekend I was scheduled to teach in Barcelona, Spain. It was cancelled, of course, and as the rest of world also went into lockdown, I decided to teach the seminar online for free. What followed is a story for another time, but I will try to condense it into one precise sentence. The past two years have been dreadful, yet wonderful, exhilarating and truly an innovative period of my career; a real karate adventure. Taking these chances is a vital way to keep my karate alive. As I said before, karate is austere and mundane. The constant honing of skills, conditioning of the body and building of mental resilience is, frankly, tedious. If that was the entirety of my karate life, I am not sure I would have lasted so long. No, part of my training has always been, as my good friend Simon Bligh puts it, having karate adventures.

What is a karate adventure? Well, the obvious ones are the trips away. When I was a kid, on holiday with my parents, I would always take my dogi. We would find the nearest library (long before the World Wide Web made an appearance) to check out their club listings. Calls would be made, and my loving family would sacrifice one of their precious nights on holiday to sit in a local parish hall and watch me train. It was great. I never knew what I was heading into, but without exception, I walked out of the newly discovered dojo with a smile on my face and in receipt of a 'you're welcome back anytime' farewell. I feel it should be part of every dojo ethos, to reach out, make connections and have adventures.

Having studied anthropology at university, I know there is hard data and good research around this idea. We are social animals and thrive when we are part of a solid, well-structured community, but we thrive best when that community has good connections to other groups. For primitive man, that was the neighbouring village where they made alliances, trading, marrying and working together when needed. Now, with technology, that same tendency to connect with other communities has only been limited by the speed of one's internet connection. The literal web that has been created by the metaphorical web is as strong and real as those that have existed from the dawn of civilisation, and this should be capitalised on.

I have taught at many dojo throughout the world over the decades. Some stand out. They are popular, well run, and bursting with members. Part of their ethos is to invite visiting instructors and plan adventures – that is how I get to know them; sometimes I am the adventure! These normally take the shape of an annual summer camp. Same place, same time each year, it becomes a ritual that the majority of the members take part in. From the outside, there may be a lot of well-it's-all-right-for-them-isms: they have a big dojo, they have many members, they can afford to do that etc. Yet for me, these naysayers have it backwards. The large membership does not facilitate the karate adventures, the karate adventures produce the large membership. Without doubt, there is a large dollop of faith needed to hurl oneself, as a dojo instructor, into the quagmire of event organisation.

But I can only talk from my own experience. Setting up the JKS GB & Ireland in October of 2002 I immediately invited Kagawa Sensei, the then technical director of the JKS, to teach a seminar for my fledging group. We held it in Nottingham, UK, nowhere near the two existing dojo that had already affiliated to the JKS GB.

Faith and naivety won the day and the event was a huge success. By the end of the three-day event, the JKS GB & Ireland had more than doubled in size. It was the start of an uninterrupted decade of spring and autumn JKS GB & Ireland Technical Seminars, Kagawa Sensei coming each spring and another top instructor visiting in the autumn. People wanted these adventures, whether they knew it or not, and each year built upon the last.

On a local level, whether a dojo is inviting a visiting sensei to teach, organising a weekend gasshuku or simply travelling up the road on a Monday night to train with a dojo you have never met before, having karate adventures puts you on a journey; boredom is alleviated and sustainability is achieved. As the saying goes, 'If you want to go fast, go alone. If you want to far, go together.' The sustainable karate journey is, hopefully, a long one. Better travel with as wide a community as possible and, bringing it back to the start of this idea, the pandemic did just that. The past two years have been tough to the core, yet the adventure I had was breathtaking – only marred by the price we all had to pay for it. My point is, the fun of having the karate adventure is the superficial wrapping of something far more important. Whether we travel up the road to a new dojo on halfway around the world to an international seminar, we face the unknown. In one way or another, at the essence of anything we use to better ourselves is the process of having to face the unknown. We don't go to school or university to study ideas we already know. Karate must be the same. A karate adventure is a self-orchestrated quest, a self-imposed challenge, a chance to test one's mettle. I find this an essential approach to my practice. It produces a dynamic, forever-changing approach to training, to thinking, to being. Therefore, my journey becomes sustainable – even when I am told I have to stay at home for two years!

Having adventures. Drinking hot cocktails at the Snow Festival in Hokkaido, Japan.

EIGHT

Don't be myopic

'I do karate.'

'I do Shotokan karate.'

'I do JKA Shotokan karate.'

'I do Hombu Dojo JKA Shotokan karate.'

'I do Naka Sensei's Hombu Dojo JKA Shotokan karate.'

People competing over who does the best karate, they think it's a race to the top …

I once had a very pleasant evening with Steve Arneil Sensei, the Kyokushin Karate pioneer, who promoted that style of karate throughout Europe after spending four tough years in Japan. We bonded over far too many pints and spoke about our shared experiences of the country. It amazed me when he told me that in 1961, he arrived at Japan and there wasn't really a strong sense of different styles. Of course, each famous instructor had their own school and taught their own brand, but things were far more fluid back then – and I liked the idea of that. He had visited the JKA Hombu and trained with Nakayama Sensei. 'It wasn't tough enough for me,' he said. 'I wanted a little more.' Jeez, I thought, this old guy in front of me must have been one crazy SOB, back in the day. He was great! Oyama Sensei's dojo in Ikebukuro had been suggested to him, so off he went, and the rest is famous Kyokushin Karate history.

Back then, the fluid, almost dynamic nature of karate schools was reflected by how people thought about what they did. Karate was a tool, a process, a mould that allowed transformation of oneself into something other – a karate-ka. Now, I fear, it isn't quite like that. The necessary formation of associations and federations has facilitated many great areas of growth within karate worldwide, but at the same time has solidified other aspects. Layer upon layer of filtering, sifting and purifying in order to standardise technique has produced a distilled version of what was. In many cases, this has been terrific. The athleticism, the speed, power and precision that all good karate-ka now superficially outshine our counterparts of the past. Yet behind that veneer of acceptability I often feel there are an awful lot of karate-ka that are protected from the reality of budo by the badge they wear or the instructor they train with. Has too much functionality been lost due to the quest of a standardised, acceptable form?

Facebook and Instagram are awash with profile pictures of the famous group logos, accompanied by the three-lettered acronyms, or the person the profile represents standing proudly next to their famous instructors; as if either of these things emit glorious energy, allowing the profile-owner to bathe in reflective legitimacy.

I can often see that this reflective legitimacy is used as a carapace for many, elevating the recipients in status and standing within their chosen community. However, the inevitable conclusion of such ways is a myopic view of what karate is and what it can be.

Imagine a karate-ka identifying strongly with a certain instructor. I use the example of the JKA's Naka Sensei above, only because I think he is brilliant. I trained with him a long time ago, on the East Fire Dojo 1992 Summer Gasshuku in Chiba. Little did I know he had just won the All-Japan Championships. Yet when we paired up during dojo kumite, he was kind, supportive and patient with this nineteen-year-old kid flailing about in front of him. So I use him as an example because he is very worthy of all the adulation that is heaved upon him.

When someone is revered like that, it is common to see their students follow to the letter what is taught. After all, imitation is the sincerest form of flattery. But if we quote Oscar Wilde in his entirety, what he actually said was *Imitation is the sincerest form of flattery that mediocrity can pay to greatness*. He was clearly speaking about karate.

As instructors, I am sure we hope that our students find their own path. Following in the sensei's footsteps is fine for a certain time, yet it would be such a shame for someone to think they are on their own journey only to realise too late that they have simply cut and pasted their instructor's unique path into their own lives. Most of the time this is not the fault of the instructor. Many students relax and revel in the comfort of following someone else to the letter – it removes the need to flex the grey-matter muscles when training. Karate-ka following this path can become institutionalised, comforted by the absolute knowledge of what to expect and what is expected of them. They can become myopic in their view of what is good karate and what isn't. And the more reassurance and comfort they feel they need about their own karate, the more myopic they become. This can develop to a point where a millimetre either side of the one correct truth means that everything is wrong.

Compare that to the experience that Steve Arneil Sensei

had. At that time, no one was legitimised by another, everyone was proving themselves in the dojo, to their sensei, to fellow students, to themselves. If what they were doing worked, then it was of value; if it didn't, it wasn't. Without being too rose-tinted about the past, I believe karate was far simpler, honest and (arguably) valuable back then. To become a karate-ka, you had to work for it, and keep working for it. Credibility was not automatically bestowed simply by wearing the correct badge or having the correct acronym after your rank. Karate ability hadn't descended to simply the ability to remember the count of each kata or having the correct tie that represents your referee rank or remembering the latest Hombu Dojo kata updates – as if it were vital to know that the group now do the first movement of Jitte in shomen, rather than hanmi. And failure to know this would crash the whole system of one's authority and credibility. Give me a break!

Being a sustainable karate-ka is about taking knowledge and inspiration from all instructors, all styles, even all physical pursuits where excellence is achieved. We cannot allow ourselves to become myopic and hope it will last. Being focused on a minute part of the spectrum of what karate can be is unimaginative, trite and the furthest possible distance away from what could be considered dynamic. What's more, allowing the imposition of this blinkered vision of what karate is by draconian teaching of an authoritarian instructor is the antithesis of what a sensei should be. Karate is about maximising the spectrum of possibility, opening one's hand in order to not hold on to anything, to simply let go … whatever that may be. It is a negative feedback cycle: the more focused you become on a certain way of doing something, the more you have to focus on that to ignore any contradictory evidence. I have seen it on my travels and it seems obvious to me that those around these myopic karate-ka will become disillusioned, angry and, ultimately, alienated from the sensei or group they once associated with.

As a small aside, I often think that this is closely related to the physicality of the person. I have noticed, with little exception, that those who are physically stiff, who find that stretching has little payback, often end up having a similar mental approach. Equally, those who are flexible, naturally elastic and react quickly to any stretching routine are often flexible in their psychological make-up. I think I fall into this latter category. I have always been flexible, easily able to stretch into most positions and shapes – and perhaps, as a consequence, I am often adaptable to the organisational situations I face. As I have mentioned before, being in a position of leadership means that, more often than not, you end up allowing stuff to go on that you don't necessarily agree with and I still stand by that, knowing I am more prone to being agreeable.

In opposition, those who aren't physically flexible often have stiff thinking. They rule their dojo or group with an iron fist, maybe scoring low on agreeableness or even empathy. I think either approach is ultimately limited. Just like our karate, where sometimes we must be supple and giving and, sometimes, we must be tense and unaccommodating, so too, must we be mentally like that. Too draconian, no one will follow you. Too accommodating, everyone will walk over you. Balance, like everything in life, is crucial.

Smiling after enjoying a class with Paolo Bolaffio Sensei.

NINE

Karate isn't a thing; a karate-ka is

I remember the first time I trained with Rick Jackson Sensei. It was the spring of 2017 and meeting him was a welcome breath of fresh air during a period of upheaval in my karate career. 'What is karate?' he said while we were being drilled with ido kihon. 'Show me! Where is it? Can you see it?' I stopped myself from shrugging, unsure what to reply to this possibly trick question. 'Karate isn't a thing,' he continued just in the nick of time. 'We create karate every moment we train, we move, we do.'

I smiled, thinking, I really like this guy.

Several years earlier I was teaching in Cincinnati with Rick Hotton Sensei. At the end of our joint session, the busy dojo gathered around for an informal Q&A.

'For both sensei, what does practising Shotokan karate mean for you?' came the first question.

Rick looked over to me and gave a look that left no doubt that he was passing the buck. Okay, here goes, I thought.

'Well …' I gathered my thoughts while trying to judge the audience. 'I don't really think I do Shotokan.' There was a slight murmur, but nothing major. It spurred me on. 'In fact, I don't even think I do karate.' That was received less well, but at least it was received. I continued. 'I think mostly, I just turn up and be me.'

I looked over at Rick to see him give one of those inverted smiles – bottom lip pushed up, cheeks pulled down – while nodding in agreement. 'Sure, Shotokan is the language we use to communicate our ideas, but it isn't really anything.' I could still feel I hadn't brought everyone on board yet. I persevered. 'Take any word. The word "word", for example. The sounds don't have any intrinsic meaning other than what we give them. All English-speakers have agreed that the sounds made when you say "word" means that pre-arranged concept of the idea of word.'

Admittedly, it was all a bit 'paralysis through analysis', but it was a point worth making. I think most of them got it and Rick and I were able to leave the dojo without being burnt as heretics; luckily it wasn't one of 'those' dojo!

But why is it that this even needs to be pointed out? Do we look at the London Underground map and think all the routes are straight lines, interspersed by deadly ninety-degree turns? Do we think dragging a file icon on our laptop into the recycle bin means that is actually happening somewhere in the bowels of our computer? Do we really think that the money in our pockets has any intrinsic value, rather than it simply being a desperately ageing fiat system that was doomed the moment the gold standard was dropped and the dollar was linked to oil, just as the resource peaked? I digress.

My point is that the world is full of useful fictions, axiomatic truths that we apply to make sense of the environment and our place in it. Karate is no different. When we start training, it is all shapes and counts, strictly dictated by the sensei. I, and many great sensei long before me, have concluded that this little fiction is the best way to become a martial artist; all alternatives throw up their own unique downsides and drawbacks. The downside of Shotokan's way is that the shapes and counts that we use to teach can often become prisons from which the students are unable to break free. This pedagogy reinforces the idea that karate is a noun, a thing to acquire, something, that once gained, cannot be lost. This leads to making the mistake in thinking that the training mechanisms of karate is karate itself.

Karate is a verb, not a noun.

I taught in Romania a few years ago. A wonderful, talented group that I was meeting for the first time. They had a full-time dojo with a makiwara in the corner. Halfway through the first class, I was discussing where one's focus should be in a technique, when someone said, 'Surely it should be the point of kime – at the end.'

'Okay,' I said, 'where is the strongest part of the technique? For example, gyaku zuki?'

'At the end,' came the universal answer, as I walked over to the makiwara.

'Really?' I hit the makiwara, making contact almost at the end of the technique. It was strong and they all nodded, with an *osu*. I then nudged a little closer and blasted the striking board, hitting it midway through the trajectory of the punch.

'Ooh …' came the response.

I am sure I followed my vain display with an unfathomable explanation of the bell curve of muscle strength and the synchronisation of the impact phase of each element of the technique, but I concluded with, 'Have you ever seen a boxer knock someone out?' Of course, they had. It was part of the collective knowledge of the whole group, yet they had never put the two together: the knowledge that we practise gyaku zuki, allowing the arm to fully extend, and the fact that boxers knock their opponents out with a bent arm.

I best leave for another day the discussion about form vs function and the benefits of practising either aspect during our martial arts training. But what is important is the understanding that whatever aspect we are practising, we are just practising a training method. A sprinter practises with a parachute on her back. A baseball player warms up with a metal 'doughnut' around his bat before he goes out to hit. And a karate-ka practises kihon in a long, exaggerated stance. At no point should anyone think that the only way to run fast, hit a ball or make power is connected to the way we practise and train our bodies. Believing that the kata, kihon and kumite we practise in the dojo is karate is a mistake. Believing that there is such a thing as karate is a mistake. Allowing these concepts to invade our approach to training will initially help progress but will ultimately be detrimental to one's development.

What I have written above may seem oxymoronic. How

can I dedicate my life to something I don't believe exists? Yet for me, it is the ultimate freedom that karate has given me. I am no longer bound to a sensei, an organisation, a style, a certain way of doing something, a strict thought-process. The ability to go beyond the system is the ultimate gift of the system. While still truly valuing the system as a process, the sustainable approach to doing karate is to realise it isn't a thing. My rank, my status, my organisation are all make-believe. The only thing that matters is, How capable am I? Have I fulfilled my potential?

TEN

Axiomatic judgement

I often post videos online; you may have noticed … Mostly, I am happy to say, I get positive feedback. After all, what is social media for if not to boost one's ego? However, the one type of video that I can guarantee will bring those trolls out from under their cyber bridges are videos about kata bunkai. 'That'll never work!' is normally the tamest of comments, while most deteriorate rapidly southwards from this point. Generally speaking, I just delete the comments; occasionally I engage. Yet when people are speaking two different languages, the chances of a productive outcome are slender at best. The problem is, both are literally speaking a different language. Maybe the words that we use are both English, but the concepts that we are using the words to describe are different. We don't have a shared narrative.

For a practitioner of the grappling martial arts, the idea of standing up at a medium- to long-range distance and exchanging punches and kicks is ridiculous. 'That'll never work!' you can hear them say. 'All fights quickly go to the ground, practising strikes are waste of time!'

For a practitioner of the striking martial arts, the idea of taking someone to the ground is ridiculous. 'That'll never work!' they will mutter. 'You're going to take someone to the ground, onto concrete, onto a curb, a lamp post, onto God's knows what, while his mates, who are standing about, are ready to kick your head in as soon as they get a chance?'

For a practitioner of the energy-based martial arts, the idea of doing any full-contact training is ridiculous. 'That'll never work!' they will think. 'The ultimate self-defence is looking after one's body, not destroying it through combat training.'

We all have our own set of ideas about and requirement of our martial arts training. Each style attracts a certain type of individual that identifies with the system. Or perhaps the system produces people that identify with the style. It is a chicken-and-egg-type discussion. Ultimately, most people go to the nearest dojo or a dojo they have seen advertised. Most don't actively engage in finding out what best suits them and then seek the best dojo that teaches that style. I am sure there is some automatic selection process going on, where those best geared to that style stick it out, and the rest transition into another style or quit, never to try martial arts again. Either way, by the time they get to the point where they are arguing on the internet, they are surely engrained into one way of thinking. Once we are in that position, not matter how real-life/traditional/healthy/functional/artistic their practice is, it is most likely stagnant.

Let me use the example of kata bunkai, as mentioned earlier.

'That'll never work!' I read.

Yes, of course, I want to answer. Please, don't drop your coffee mug in shock. Let me explain.

I have studied with some great karate-ka, some of whom are just amazing when it comes to kata application. Ideas and function seem to come to them in some stream of collective unconscious. In Steve Ubl's case, attacks aren't even set up. In his Minnesotan/Southern California drawl, he simply says 'attack'. The victim initiates their own demise, throws an attack and they are suddenly on the floor, Steve Sensei having done some element of the kata. Even videos I have posted of Steve Sensei elicit the same response. Or maybe a more subdued response of 'I wouldn't do it that way, it would be much better if blah, blah, blah …'

No! I want to scream. The point is, in karate we are artificially restricting ourselves by the form with the understanding that we are practising the application of a certain section of that kata. We are literally breathing meaning into old form, giving life to what could be seen as a sterile system, sanitised by countless competitions, gradings and technical committee decisions. So, yes, that would never work. But what also would not work is taking someone hard to the ground and splitting your head open on a curb. What also wouldn't work is spending countless hours punching bags at close range, while ducking and diving only for some guy to low-kick you and snap your ACL. What also would not work is spending a lifetime connecting with your body and pushing chi from meridian point to meridian point, only for you to be mugged on the way home from your local community centre … And ultimately, nothing will work when someone pulls a gun on you.

Yet we don't have to be the strongest in the world and be able to fight off a marauding group of braggarts. To be a martial artist, we simply have to be better/stronger/faster than most people in our peer group. If you are a young lad in your twenties, then yes, you should be doing a lot of 'live' training, mixing it up, challenging yourself to become combatively strong. If you are a middle-aged woman new to martial arts, then maximising your fitness and strength, while learning basic awareness and self-defence skills, may be your goal. And if you are a retiree, new to martial arts, then maybe the movement and body connection that tai chi teaches is perfect.

What is never productive and should not be acceptable is to look over at another person and judge them on the values and decisions that you have made about your own journey. I realised that a major element of becoming a sustainable karate-ka is to accept that karate does not have all the answers and that I should actively look elsewhere for ideas and inspiration and allow it to inform my own practice; while at the same time valuing the system I 'grew up' in, since that has given me the physical intelligence to recognise and appreciate quality in others. And, as Robert Pirsig described in *Lila: An Inquiry Into Morals*, it is this dynamic quality, this ability to recognise quality in any place and not be fixated on our own myopic sense of what is good, that is vital for one's development. It starts with the complete understanding of one system, which will allow us to see the quality in all systems.

HDKI Headquarters' teaching team training with Paolo Sensei, Italy 2021.

ELEVEN

Have a good foundation

In the past, I have written a lot about how post-modern thought has infiltrated the karate world. Years of overbearing, draconian organisations have stifled and suppressed karate-ka into compliance until eventually there were great swathes of people rejecting the communities they grew up in. With only one model of management, those who left created new groups, but in the image of the ones they had rejected. The result: split after split, fracture after fracture. Eventually, you could almost hear the collective sigh and the muttering of 'What's the point?'

What grew from that was a certain nihilism. Grades seemed arbitrary and pointless. Classic training methods, kihon drills, even kata practice was questioned and (in some cases) also rejected. A number of years ago, a friend called me. 'I am going to give myself godan,' he announced. He was a very credible yondan, a rank he had received from a reputable international group.

'What … how … why?' I settled on why being the most salient question.

'The guy down the road is godan and I need the high grade to attract students.'

'Oh,' I said. I considered saying that when joining my dojo no one has ever asked my grade or the grade of any of the five instructors who teach for me. I did consider telling him that the vast majority of people just join the closest dojo or the dojo they see the advert for. I did consider telling him that it is highly unlikely that any beginner will even consider what martial art they are going to try, let alone the grade of the instructor. Instead, I just said, 'Well, why don't you make yourself rokudan?'

'What?'

'In fact, if it is just about attracting students, make yourself hachidan. What's the difference?'

'Don't be ridiculous!' he replied.

It is all ridiculous, though. I am sure there are some people reading this now saying, 'No, not me! I have my rank from XYZ, or ABC or OMG.' They will condemn those who promote themselves, unaware that the very fact that they put so much worth into the origin of their Dan certificate pushed people into this post-modern, nihilistic world in the first place. The solution: simply focus on your foundation.

Karate is a martial art. Art always evolves and changes. From music to theatre to sculpture to martial, everything has changed over time. It is a delicate balance between tradition and innovation, and it is in this space that the true art of karate is found. But before we destroy and denigrate our system, we need to understand it.

Pablo Picasso is famous in the arts world for co-founding the cubist movement and known elsewhere for painting people with eyes in the wrong place. Many, I am sure, have asked whether he could really paint – after all, some of his paintings look somewhat simple. Yet anyone with the slightest knowledge of art will know he was a creative genius and an exceptionally skilled artist. Google some of his early work and you will see portraits he painted with such talent that it boggles the mind to think he would change his style the way he did, later on in his career.

Picasso kindly provides me with the example of the need for a good foundation. A number of years ago, I was friendly with a group of dojos that had banded together to form an informal association. The seniors consisted of a few Nidans and one Sandan. They formed a technical committee and set about standardising kata and ensuring that those who passed their gradings were technically proficient. On the surface, I thought it was a somewhat admirable solution to the issues that arose when they were forced to leave the association that they had grown up in. For good or bad, no longer did they have their Japanese instructor looming over them. It was only when I started teaching that the unintended consequences arose. I began with Tekki Shodan. 'Oh, we don't do it that way,' one of the seniors interrupted my class.

'What way?' There is little interpretation of Tekki Shodan in the Shotokan world.

'Well, the nami ashi – we don't do that anymore.'

'Really?' My look asked for more information.

'Well, it makes no sense. So, we dropped it.'

I was the guest. They were my hosts. I respected their position and left it at that, allowing them to perform the kata as they saw fit – after all, that really was not the focus of the class anyway. The point is, 'not making sense' and 'not making sense for them' are two very distinct things. All too often I have seen karate-ka make decisions based on flawed or insufficient information. To paraphrase Dave Hopper, they think they are following the way but instead end up down a cul-de-sac.

I, too, find myself in a position where I have left those instructors who were so influential on my journey. I understand the difficulty of being out alone, in the karate wilderness. And despite having a very solid foundation, laid down over many years of training in Japan and before that with Kato Sadishige Sensei, I never thought I could technically stand on my own. I always sought out high-calibre instructors that I could at least bounce ideas off or, hopefully, have them critique my technique or classes. This works in academia all the time. Of course, we may have heard stories of tenured professors who came up with good theories decades earlier. Then, despite mounting contradictory evidence, they continue to defend their position at all costs. Thankfully, I am sure this is very rare. When functioning correctly, the peer-reviewed process of academia is amazing. Experts in their chosen field toil away at research, produce papers, ideas and theories, aiming to have them published in peer-reviewed publications. That peer-reviewing process, however, is the gauntlet they must battle through. Their concepts are challenged, scrutinised, torn down if they are weak or left standing if their foundations are strong. This is how I see my process. Ultimately, what I am looking for, what I am desperately trying to do, is to avoid stagnation. Regurgitating and spewing out the same classes week after week, month after month, numbs the brain of the instructor and student alike. With a solid foundation, and a solid feedback network, I find it easy to be open-minded, rather than shut off and prone to rejecting something I don't understand. For me, this is the sustainable way forward.

Have a good foundation.

TWELVE

Teach to the generation below

All too many of my stories start with 'I was once having a pint with …'

I was once having a pint with a very senior instructor within the British karate scene. He was a rokudan, maybe nanadan at the time and was late in his fifties, maybe even early sixties. I liked him. He was still strong, flexible and sprightly. He had attended many of the seminars that I had been teaching in the UK at the time and although not part of the association I was with, was very friendly towards it.

We sat, post-training, as he lamented about the situation of his own dojo. 'I'm just sick of teaching white belt kids,' he said.

'Sure.' At the time, during the week, that is all I was doing. But this guy was twenty-five, maybe thirty, years older than me. I couldn't image having to endlessly demonstrate Heian Shodan and say things like 'right leg forward … no, your other right leg forward' to the same demographic a quarter of a century in the future.

'I've been doing it so long,' he continued. 'I think I may just give up.'

'You can't do that,' I said, in a knee-jerk response. 'You

can't quit karate.'

'No, no.' He waved his hand. 'I'm just going to quit teaching.'

I am not sure if he did. I hope he didn't. And if he did, I hope he still managed to continue training. Over the next year or so he slowly stopped coming to seminars and I haven't heard anything about him since. But I clearly remember that I completely agreed with him. Someone who has been training for maybe the best part of fifty years should not be responsible for teaching white-belt kids.

In fact, I am a firm believer that really you are only going to truly appeal to those of your own generation and maybe one generation below. When I first started my dojo, I was twenty-nine years old and the vast majority of the adults I attracted were also in their twenties. As I meandered through my thirties, my original students grew older with me, but also new students who joined were a similar age. By the time I found myself in my forties, I was attracting very few students in their twenties, and it was only when I employed a couple of younger instructors that we started to get similarly young students. Now, my dojo boasts about 650 students. The average age must be somewhere in the early teens. We have loads of young children, but close to a hundred-strong adult base, yet the two classes I teach are mostly populated by the adults in their thirties and forties. We have instructors in their twenties, but their classes are populated by the younger adults in our group – and for me, that is just fine. In fact, I would argue that is the way it should be.

Obviously, as we get older our focus and interest change. Hopefully, they develop and evolve as we make our way through our karate journey. Subtly or demonstrably, this affects our teaching. I watch some of my younger instructors teach in the dojo or at seminars and they teach the nuts and bolts of karate. They break down kata, invent *kihon* sequences or play about with *kumite* drills. I recognise it, because that is what I used to do – although I hope theirs is more evolved. What I teach and focus on now is different. My interests have moved on, developed in a direction that is less about the nuts and bolts of karate and more about 'other stuff'. However, we neglect what my younger instructors are teaching at our peril. The younger instructors are much closer to the needs and wants of the younger students, so for an older instructor to dominate all teaching (whether it be a large, professional dojo or a small community dojo) can be very limiting. Junior instructors may feel unvalued, younger adults may feel bored. The end result may be the senior instructor being left with only white-belt kids to teach and that will get boring very quickly.

That said, Oyama Sensei, founder of Kyokushin, famously taught a white-belt class each week at their Hombu Dojo in Ikebukuro. He insisted that this was as important for any instructor: to stay connected to the beginning of people's journeys. I agree.

I occasionally get white-belt adults turning up to my class. My Monday classes are for seniors only. My Thursday classes are open to all, although my secretary tries to dissuade beginners from joining that class as there are many other options. Occasionally one does slip through the invisible net and stumbles into my class. 'Who's that?' I'll ask my other instructors who often join my training.

'It's Bob/Sally/Alex … they've just joined … Be nice!' They will berate me before I have even said a word. And they are right, of course. I am not a tyrant in my class, but I am too used to teaching seniors. Teaching juniors and beginners is a vital part of the process but to make that process sustainable, making sure the dojo is future-proofed and having young, enthusiastic instructors is vital.

And this brings me on to my second but connected point. We must be good sempai.

I wrote an article years ago called 'The Sempai-Kohai Relationship'. It was my reaction to coming home after my time in Japan (I don't want to regurgitate it here as I am sure it is online somewhere). My basic premise was that in Japan, when going out with sempai, a good kohai would take care of them. The kohai would do all the ordering of food, pouring of drink, fetching of shoes, carrying of bags. As a kohai, we were there to facilitate the night. Then, at the end of the night, the sempai would quietly pay the bill and announce the evening was at an end. We would thank them with deep bows, and we all went home happy.

Arriving back in the UK, I went out with a sempai who, used to the culture in Japan (or so I thought), expected and received the same treatment. The one difference: when, at the end of the night, the bill arrived, he took it from the waitress and said, 'Right, shall we just split it 50/50?'

He is a very good guy, but this is not the action of a good sempai.

Being a good sempai is about paying it forward, a never-ending spiral of mutually supportive sempai and kohai. Yet cycles can be ended by one person jumping out of the loop. I think it is exceptionally important to take care of those who are in your charge. Of course, that could be the easy option of giving them money, but of far more value is one's time, trust and knowledge. Using the example of above, giving a junior instructor one's time, trust and knowledge – even money – to help them teach and develop as an instructor, future-proofs one's dojo. I often think of the senior sensei who used to attend my seminars. If he had focused on helping to mentor and nurture young instructors, would he have been in the situation he faced when I last saw him? An answer to that would only be speculation. Even back then I remember thinking I don't want to risk that possibility. One of the underlying principles of the HDKI is to provide opportunity, for this very reason. And as a sustainable karate-ka, I think it is fundamentally important to secure one's training environment. If we don't have a dojo to go to, a schedule to keep to and a community to be responsible for, then all other efforts to maintain one's karate could be in vain.

Teaching in Crimea, Ukraine in 2008.

THIRTEEN

Having an inefficient, sustainable system

It is much better to have a system that achieves 80 per cent of your goals but is 100 per cent doable than a system that achieves 100 per cent of your goals but is only 80 per cent doable. This is a rule I have basically lived my life by. And at the heart of that rule is *being appropriately lazy by just doing enough!*

From my school days, I did just enough. At GCSE level (exams taken at sixteen years old), no one really expected me to go on to higher education, but I did just enough to qualify for sixth form. At eighteen, no one really expected me to go to university, but my A levels were just good enough to go to Keele University, conveniently located sixteen miles from Kato Sadishige Sensei's dojo. At university, no one really knew me in the geography or anthropology departments, but I had set myself a goal of gaining a 2:1 (I had heard it was a drinking man's First) and surprised both academic departments by achieving just that – even though I spelt 'geogaphy' wrong on my dissertation. In the final tally, I had three papers over 70 per cent and an average of 65.1 per cent – I needed three papers over 70 per cent and an average of above 65 per cent to get a 2:1. I had done just enough and headed to Japan, ready for a different challenge and finding new ways to do the bare minimum.

My goal, consciously or subconsciously, was always to achieve what I wanted but to attain those goals with the least possible effort. Some may baulk as such a statement – achieving something with the least possible effort sounds like the utterance of a charlatan or a scallywag. However, 'least possible effort' does not mean little effort. In fact, in most cases it was quite the opposite. My time at university and in Japan was tough. I trained religiously, but I never overdid it. And, I think it has stood me in good stead. I have already mentioned that I was influenced early on by seeing people who no longer had that fire in their belly that I still have. I wasn't naive enough to think that 'that will never happen to me'. In fact, I very easily convinced myself that if it happened to them, it was definitely going to happen to me. So I set about playing the long game.

Well before I had read or watched anything of Simon Sinek and his ideas of the infinite game,[1] I simply paced myself, allowing for the occasional failure. Earlier, I mentioned meeting Steve Arneil Sensei. The reason our paths crossed was that I had been invited to the thirtieth anniversary of the Irish Karate Kyokushin, the full-contact karate organisation in Ireland. It was a great event with a room full of tough people.

1. Simon Sinek is a mostly British, but also American author who, amongst other books, wrote *The Infinite Game*. That book's basic synopsis is that in business (and I think karate and life) we shouldn't be playing finite games, where we are looking at winning short-term strategies, but instead play the infinite game, understanding that the rules are constantly changing, there is an unknown number of players and the only goal is to stay in the game for as long as possible.

At one point during the evening they asked the senior instructors to come up on stage to receive presents and awards. Most were in their sixties and had achieved ranks of rokudan and above. Not one of them skipped up the steps and most looked like they struggled with hip and knee problems. Now, you can see similar issues with long-standing Shotokan seniors, although maybe not with the same frequency. My experience in Japan was no different. My sempai on the instructors' course all had one issue or another due to over-training. This was somehow par for the course, but as Rick Hotton Sensei is fond of saying, the best self-defence is looking after our own bodies. What's the point in dedicating oneself to karate-do only to destroy the very vehicle we use on that journey? So, from an early age I was well aware of the cost/reward balance in karate. Sure, I could train mentally or physically (or both) in the extreme and achieve incredible results, but the cost ... what would the cost be? A body that is broken? A spirit that is warped? It is an expensive price to pay and sometimes self-defeating. So, probably subconsciously at first, but certainly more mindfully as time went on, I have tried to find that delicate balance between pushing forward while standing still and being in the moment. For as long as I can remember now, I have seen the importance of tapping into the drive, that insecurity, that need to train hard and be better, while occasionally looking back and realising how far I have come, how much I have accomplished. I am my worst critic and my best cheerleader. These two sides of my personality help create balance. And when I don't achieve balance, I eventually forgive myself for that too. This is my system and I have found it to be the best way to sustain my practice.

Hiking in the Wicklow Mountains with members of the Dojo.

FOURTEEN

You ain't all that, Scott!

I do yoga.

That is not the first time I have admitted to that, but I guess it is the most public admission.

I go to a very cosy place a short cycle ride from where I live. The Little Bird Café and Yoga Studio is all that you imagine. It is populated by long-haired men with earrings and women with crew cuts and tattoos … I generalise, a tad, but it is a world far away from what I am used to.

Shortly before the pandemic I made my way to the café and set about readying myself to do the normal Friday-morning class. Waiting for our normal, talented and usually punctual instructor, the class was surprised when in walks a new instructor. She was young, Lycra-clad and oozed the Italian sexiness that her name (Fabiana) suggested. We set about slowly getting ready for the hour of stretching, contorting and connecting with our bodies. I am usually the only male in the class and, more often than not, the most flexible and able; thankfully, yoga is not a competitive sport, otherwise I would be reigning champion, having vanquished the competition of middle- to late-aged ladies that join me in the studio.

Halfway through the session, Fabiana had taken an

interest in my practice, giving me more and more elaborate and advanced positions to strive for. I always like a challenge, even in yoga. Like an irritating child at the front of class, I revelled in being teacher's pet and pushed on. At one point Fabiana had instructed us into the Half Lord of Fishes pose. For me, though, she suggested the Full Lord of Fishes pose. I made the necessary adjustments and twisted, rotated and squeezed into position. It's part of my regular warm-up stretching routine anyway, so not so challenging. But sitting upright as my right leg was bent, laid flat in front of me with my right heel pulled back to my left buttock, and my left leg was up and bent over my other leg, with the left foot pulled across and beside my right thigh, Fabiana decided my upper body wasn't twisting enough. She came behind me, put her arms around my shoulders and chest, anchored my feet with her legs and slowly rotated me clockwise. It was at this point I let out a massive fart.

You ain't all that, Scott!

Added to that is the reason I do yoga in the first place. Back in 2017 I visited my doctor for my annual check-up. Due to slightly dodgy genes, I have been on blood-pressure medication since my early forties. This check-up and a following 24-hour blood-pressure monitor showed that my stats were still too high. At the follow-up appointment my doctor informed me he would have to up my medication.

'Oh, well,' I said, 'maybe when I am less stressed it will go down a little.' He looked up from the prescription pad he had been writing on.

'Why, what's the problem?' I told him about the recent turmoil and stress of being expelled from the WTKO via social media. How I had to suddenly regroup and create my own association. How twice, in the space of three years, I had lost everything I had worked for. He took the prescription that he'd been writing, screwed it up and threw it away.

'Listen, Scott,' – he knew me well and was very plain-talking – 'as far as I am concerned you do FUCK ALL during the day. Take up fucking yoga! Now get out of here!'

I love my doctor.

My point is, from Fabiana's point of view I am a middle-aged, farty man. From my doctor's point of view, I am a patient with a chronic issue who exacerbates it with certain life choices. Both of the lenses that they use to look at me are as equally valid as any that I can come up with and I would do well never to forget that.

You ain't all that, Scott!

From a very young age, karate was all that I ever wanted to do. That was what I did, that was who I was. Everything I approached was viewed through the lens of karate. Achieving grades at school was viewed through the lens of 'how can this help my karate?' Choosing the university was the same. My circle of friends, my interests, hobbies, pastimes were all positioned within the focus of the karate lens. I even met my wife at our university karate club. She is now a Yondan and has competed internationally. My life has been dictated to by the choice many decades ago to walk through the door of the local dojo. And I feel lucky and privileged to have found my passion, a lens to help focus my life, at such an early age. Some people are not so lucky. They may meander through life without any real journey. I will be forever grateful that I found my path very early on.

Still, there is an inherent danger in using such a narrow bandwidth to view our own lives. I have met, read and watched many great people who have many great ideas in the karate world and learnt countless lessons from them. The issue I often find, though, is the greater the idea they have, the stronger the lens they use to view the karate world, the more insular they become. One moment of brilliance is allowed to impact every aspect of their journey. We can easily see this when styles compare themselves with each other, I have written about this earlier. But beyond those ego-driven cross-style rivalries, we can see the same within styles. Shotokan instructors who insist that the way they do it is the only correct way to do it. They exist in a self-contained bubble, an echo-chamber vibrating with the permanent *kiais* of their loyal and unquestioning students. For them, imprisoned by a polished and refined lens of their own making, everything becomes black and white, day or night. What's more, this lens can often be used to bring all of life into focus. Can I draw a line between someone winning of the All-Japan Championships back in the 1980s and the outrageously poor treatment of a young waitress in some swanky restaurant in London by the same guy forty years later? Yes, yes I think I can. It is this idea that individuals can use this small and (for most people) insignificant moment in their life, or a technical skill of a passtime 99.9999 per cent of the world don't practise to project an image of themselves that all must accept, even kowtow to.

This is fraud. This is the basis of a cult. This is the antithesis of what karate should be.

There is no black or white, day or night. Everything exists within a spectrum. Most things exits in the grey, in the dusk, in the dawn. I don't want my journey to be along an autobahn, pedal to the metal, full speed ahead. No, my journey is much more a *desire path,* those user-created routes that spring up out of nowhere on grassy quadrangles or across open playing fields. Something perks my interest, a YouTube video, an article, a visiting instructor and I will be off, hacking my way through a undiscovered route of my meandering journey. I will walk that route until it is well trodden or until I reach a dead end. At that point, with reassuring predictability, something else will pop up on the horizon and I will be off again, in search of pastures new.

As a result, the polished, focused lens through which I view my karate is constantly being replaced with a lump of glass that I have to start working on, that I have to start refining. I am exceptionally lucky to have been allowed to stand on the shoulders of many giants who allow this approach and way of being. I will be forever grateful to those who have influenced my journey. Every time I head in a new direction, I have my thesis of what karate is. More often than not, I am met with an antithesis. It is at that point I get excited, waiting for the inevitable synthesis to happen.

I have been asked what defines my karate. I don't know. I haven't finished yet, but if I had to pin it down, it is this. It is to stay on the journey for as long as possible. It is to discard what I know and to seek the unknown. It is to practise sustainable karate.

Postscript

I am too young to tell you what I really think. I am still in my forties.

I will see you again in about ten years' time when I will publish the last in my autobiographic trilogy, *Karate Adventures*.

Until then, keep on keeping on.

Scott, June 2022

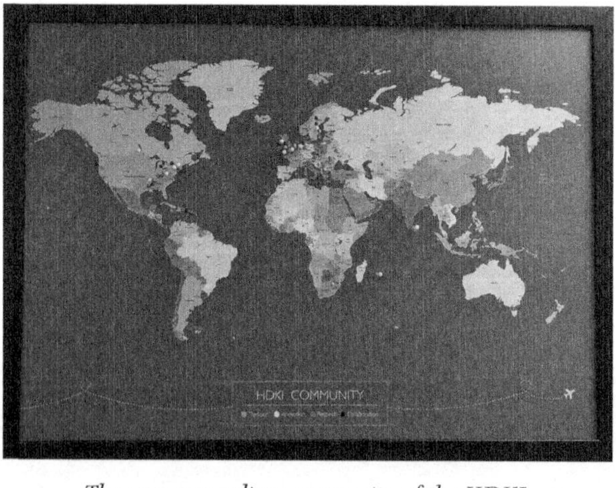

The ever-expanding community of the HDKI.

Printed in Great Britain
by Amazon

62067200R00047